Christian Memoir, Prayer, Study & Travel Journal

Publisher: Starr Publishing
StarrPublishing.com | 1-786-693-4223
Printed by Create Space
Published on: February 3, 2017
ISBN-13: 978-1542743815
ISBN-10: 1542743818
Printed in the United States of America

This Journal Belongs to

____

37588181R00084

Made in the USA
Middletown, DE
28 February 2019